孙子
SUN TZU
(c.545 BC-470 BC)

The Wisdom of China

SUN TZU
The Ultimate Master of War

By Xu Yuanxiang & Li Jing

 CHINA INTERCONTINENTAL PRESS

CONTENTS

Introduction / *9*

Born into a Military Family / *15*

Working on 'The Art of War' / *33*

Ability to Command Troops / *61*

Cream of 'The Art of War' / *79*

Destroying a Superpower / *95*

Fading from Historical Record / *109*

Quotations from Sun Tzu / *117*

計篇

曹操曰計者選將量敵度地料卒遠近險易計於朝堂也○李筌曰計者兵之上也太一遁甲先計神加德宮以斯主客成敗故孫子論兵亦以計為首○杜牧曰計算也曰計算何事曰下之五事所謂道天將法也於廟堂之上先以彼我之五事計算優劣然後勝負既定然後興師動眾用兵之道莫先此五事故為篇首耳○王晳曰計者謂計主孰天地法令兵眾賞罰也○張預曰管子曰計先定於內而後兵出境用兵之道以計為首也或曰兵貴臨敵制宜曹公謂計於廟堂者何也曰將之賢愚敵之強弱地之遠近兵之眾寡得不先計之及乎兩軍用焉變動

Introduction

On the morning of January 17, 1991, a war broke out for petroleum in the gulf area of the Middle East. For the first time, modern theories of war involving coordinated naval, air and land forces were applied to a conflict

A war broke out for petroleum in the gulf area of the Middle East in 1991.

situation, taking place in the desert. While the world was transfixed by the power of what was termed "Operation Desert Storm", a light-hearted report in *The Wall Street Journal* commented that, though China did not take part in the multi-national force, a mysterious Chinese general was in overall command of the war. He was Sun Tzu (c.545 BC - 470 BC). His masterpiece of military strategy, *The Art of War*, was being closely studied by the American marine corps as they planned their advances from the desert of Saudi Arabia. Amazingly, Sun Tzu had been dead for over 2,500 years.

During the European Football Championships in 2004, the host team, Portugal, against the odds finished as runners up. Football commentators agreed that the Portuguese team had been developing for a number of years and had some outstanding players playing in

Portrait of Sun Wu.

Europe's top leagues. However, more than one also commented on the influence of the book *The Art of War*. Portuguese coach Luiz Felipe Scolari, was a committed fan of the theories of Sun Tzu. He always carried the book in his pocket, and often quoted from it during team training.

The fact that a man and the book he wrote still exert such a profound influence over 2,500 years since his death surely makes us want to find out exactly what a kind of man Sun Tzu was and what exactly he wrote about. Of the 4,000-odd books on military strategy produced over the course of Chinese history, *The Art of War* is almost unanimously acknowledged as the most outstanding. It was written by Sun Wu (Sun Tzu), a well-known general during the late Spring and Autumn Period (770 BC-476 BC) some 2,500 years ago.

計篇

曹操曰計者選將量敵度地料卒遠近險易計於廟堂也○李筌曰計者兵之上也太一遁甲先計神加德宮以斯主客成敗故孫子論兵亦所謂計家之計法也○社牧曰計算也曰計算何事曰下之五事計筭優劣然後興師動衆用兵之道莫先此五事計勝負既定然後興師動衆用兵之道故為篇首耳○王晳曰計者謂計主將天地法令兵卒賞罰也○張預曰管子曰計先定於内而後兵出乎境故用兵之道以計為首也或曰兵貴臨敵制宜曹公謂將之賢愚敵之強弱地之遠近兵之衆

Born into a Military Family

Because no historical records exist for that time, nobody can be 100 percent certain that it was Sun Tzu who wrote *The Art of War*. Indeed we cannot even be sure that such a person really existed. If he did indeed exist, where did he come from? Historians were already debating these issues some 1,000 years ago and according to the research carried out during the Tang (618-907) and Song (960-1279) Dynasties and to genealogy records and sources in the national library, it is almost uniformly accepted Sun Tzu was born in what is now known as the town of Le'an in Huimin County, Shandong Province.

If general agreement has been reached

Born into a Military Family

Statue of Sun Wu was built in The Art of War Town of Huimin County of Shandong Province on February 21, 2006.

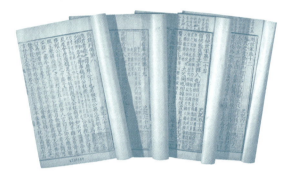

Records of the Historian.

on where Sun Tzu's place of origin is, there are countless other areas of this mysterious figure's life where the opinions of historians diverge sharply. Even the two most authoritative books on that period, *Records of the Historian* and *Spring and Autumn of Wu and Yue*, written during the Han Dynasty (206 BC-220 AD) give markedly different accounts of events and even differ on the problem as to where Sun Tzu was in fact born. Authoritative consensus seemed impossible. Then in 1972, during an archaeological excavation of a tomb at the foot of Yinque Mountain, in the Linyi area of Shandong Province, when the archeologists were sorting through the funerary objects uncovered in the tomb, they discovered a number of bamboo slips covered in writing. This writing proved to be none other than *The Art of War* and thus it was finally confirmed that *The Art of War* had indeed been produced in an age before paper had been invented. The discovery also confirmed that the author of this remarkable work was indeed none other than Sun Tzu.

These Yinque Mountain bamboo slips, which were dated to the Han Dynasty (206 BC-220 AD), in fact, contained two texts: both dealing with issues concerned with military tactics: namely, *Sun Tzu: The Art of War* and *Sun Bin: The Art of War*.

In 1972, during an archaeological excavation of a tomb at the foot of Mt. Yinque Mountain, in the Linyi of Shandong Province, archeologists discovered *Sun Tzu: The Art of War* and *Sun Bin: The Art of War*.

These two eminent strategists, who both achieved great success on the battlefield, had handed down military manuals to their offspring. The 1972 discovery was the final confirmation that Sun Tzu and Sun Bin were two different people who had written two different books, and in many ways it made things somewhat clearer for those who wished to carry out further research into the life and work of Sun Tzu and his unique contribution to Chinese and indeed global military history.

Sun Wu was born in about 535 BC in Le'an, located in what was then the Qi State, in what is now Huimin County, Shandong Province. Both his grandfather, Tian Shu, and uncle, Tian Rangju, were eminent Qi generals. The *Zuo Zhuan (Zuo's Commentary on the Spring and Autumn Annals)* contains a vivid account of a battle in which Tian Shu commanded his troops with great distinction in 523 BC. At that time he led a group of soldiers in an assault on the city walls of the enemy. Some 60 soldiers were in the process of scaling the city walls when it seemed to them that their rope had broken. They cried out in great alarm, little knowing that the whole episode had been engineered by the wily Tian Shu to spread fear among the besiegers. The plan worked perfectly and the soldiers inside the city walls fled in terror at the great clamour raised by the genuinely panicked attackers. The capture of the city without any loss of life was a significant achievement both for the Qi and for the shrewd Commander Tian Shu, who was granted an area named Le'an and invested with a new name, Sun, by the King in recognition of his services. The Qi State was a major military power during the Spring and Autumn Period (770 BC-476 BC) and with such military strength,

Born into a Military Family

Sun Wu's grandfather Tian Shu was good at fighting battles.

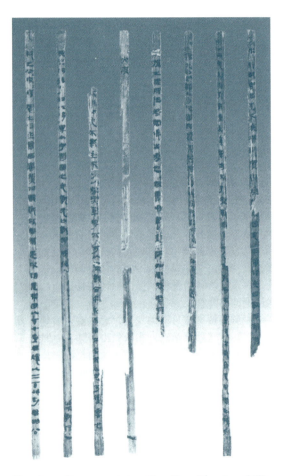

Bamboo slips containing *Sun Tzu: The Art of War* which were found from a Han Dynasty (206 BC- 220 AD) tomb at the foot of Mt. Yinqueshan in the Linyi of Shandong Province.

an advanced military culture naturally developed. For about one thousand years the Qi State maintained a preeminent position in terms of military power and influence.

Born into such a military family, Sun Tzu cannot but have been profoundly influenced by such militarily able forebears. This was, after all, the Spring and Autumn Period (770 BC-476 BC) when the major channel of education was through learning from one's immediate relatives. Undoubtedly the military background of the Sun family played a major part in the development of the young mind, who would one day write his own military masterpiece, *The Art of War.*

In contrast to the relatively peaceful Xia, Shang and Zhou Dynasties (21st century BC-256 BC)which preceded it, the Spring and Autumn Period (770 BC-476 BC) was a very warlike time. No less than 400 wars took place in slightly over 200 years. A warlike time inevitably results in every state seeking to maximize its military strength; militarism became the order of the day as each individual state looked to utilize their military might to achieve their territorial and political goals. During this turbulent period when China was being inexorably transformed into a feudal society, a veritable procession of great minds and philosophers, the greatest in Chinese history, entered the scene, as if magically summoned by the urgent imperatives of the age. Of these, Confucius, Lao Tzu and Sun Tzu are perhaps the most well-known. It is an amazing coincidence of history that the three great works which form the very foundation of Chinese traditional culture, namely *Analects of Confucius*, *Tao Te Ching* by Lao Tzu and *The Art of War* by Sun Tzu, were written by three men who lived in roughly

Lao Tzu and Confucius, two noted sages of the Spring and Autumn Period (770 BC-476 BC).

the same period.

In 1722 the French Catholic priest Joseph Amiot first introduced a European audience to *The Art of War*. Since then it has been translated into about 30 languages around the world. The English language has a well-known expression: "Business is war." Perhaps that is why so many businessmen today in America and round the world find the ancient military lessons of Sun Tzu of surprising relevance to their own 21st century careers and aspirations. They find

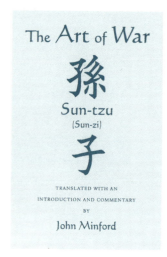

English edition of *The Art of War*.

in the ancient military manual invaluable insights into how to operate a successful business in a competitive, cut-throat environment and how to predict and adapt to future business and international trade trends.

In the U.K., *The Art of War* enjoys an equally eminent reputation. Some of its theories, strategies and tactics are still widely applied in fields such as military

Portrait of Sun Wu.

affairs and economics. Even in the most famous military colleges, special courses on *The Art of War* are being taught.

Why has such a mania for the theories of Sun Tzu developed in Western intellectual circles and indeed among common people? One significant reason is that Sun Tzu represents an authentic Oriental worldview. With the increasing integration of the world economy and development

A stone tablet inscribed with Mao Zedong's inscriptions reading: "One who knows the enemy and knows himself, will not be in danger in a hundred battles."

of what has become known as the "global village," both Chinese and foreigners need to deal with each other on a scale never previously witnessed; moreover, in order for western companies to penetrate the vast potentialities of the Chinese market, they need to come to some sort of understanding of the thinking patterns of the Chinese people as well as grasping how it is that the Chinese approach and solve problems. Indeed as Sun Tzu himself observed: "One who knows the enemy and knows himself, will not be in danger in a hundred battles."

計篇

曹操曰計者選將量敵度地料卒遠近險易計於廟堂也〇李筌曰計者兵之上也太一遁甲先計神加德宫以斷主客成敗故孫子論兵亦以計為篇首法也於廟堂之上先以彼我之五事計筭優劣然後興師動衆用兵之道莫先此五事故為篇首耳〇王晢曰計者謂計主將天地法令兵衆賞罰也〇張預曰管子曰計先定於內而後兵出境故用兵之道以計為首也或曰兵貴臨敵制宜曹公謂計

○杜牧曰計筭也曰計筭何事曰下之五事所謂道天

計者

Working on "The Art of War"

When Sun Tzu reached the age of 18, an incident occurred which would alter the entire course of his life. His uncle Tian Rangju, the Dasima of the Qi State (a position that would effectively equate to that of Board of Defense in today's world), lost his eminent position as a result of intrigues and power struggles and died of a subsequent illness. Inevitably Sun Tzu and his grandfather were affected by the fallout from Tian Rangju's fall from power.

In 517 BC, Sun Tzu, not yet 20 years old, was forced to leave his home. He chose to move to another militarily strong state, the State of Wu, in the southern lands of China. Turning his eyes one last time to gaze on

Sun Tzu was sad to leave his hometown in the Qi State.

his homeland, the young Sun Tzu must surely have recalled the joyful days spent with his family. What feelings of longing and regret must have crept over the young man as he embarked on an uncertain future accompanied only by his own shadow? The happiness and peace Sun Tzu had known in Le'an would fade forever into the bleak lakes and mountains of the lands of the State of Qi.

A tribe known as the Jingman lived in that area around 3,000 years ago, during the Western Zhou Dynasty (11th century BC-771 BC). It is a land of sunshine and abundant rain. In later times, two uncles of Zhou King Wenwang came to the area and made an enormous impact on the development of the Jingman, introducing better strains of seed and new farming techniques from the Central Plains. The two men understandably won the allegiance and

Working on "The Art of War"

Portrait of Sun Tzu in Sun Wu Yuan in Suzhou.

support of the original inhabitants and thus became the leaders of what would become the State of Wu, but which then had only slightly over 1,000 people. Centuries later by 584 BC, Shoumeng, the 19th king of the Wu State, led his troops across the Yangtze River for the first time in battle. The army conquered the Tan State in what is now part of Shandong Province. Though the Tan State was a relatively minor territory, this military expedition of an army from south of the Yangtze River was nevertheless a profound shock to the system for the states of the Central Plains, who had till then always regarded their lands as the centre of the universe. By the late Spring and Autumn Period (770 BC-476 BC), boasting a sizable territory, a powerful army and abundant natural resources, the State of Wu had become a considerable military power in the land.

It was about 526 BC that Sun Tzu first trod upon the lands of the Wu State, around what is modern day Suzhou. A power struggle, which would be directly relevant

Streets in Suzhou are flanked by blossoming peach lowers and green willows. No wonder people say Suzhou "is one of the two paradises on the Earth." The other one is Hangzhou in Zhejiang Province.

to Sun's future career, was then in progress. Prince Guang, who had long coveted the crown, failed in his bid to seize the kingship following the death of the previous king, Yimei. The kingship passed to Guang's uncle Liao.

The ambitious prince was not to be denied however. Ten years later he entrusted one of his warriors Zhuanzhu

Suzhou in Jiangsu Province is famous for its compact gardens. Pictured here is Zhuozhengyuan Garden, the largest and the most famous of its kind in the city. It was built during the Ming Dynasty (1368-1644).

Zhuanzhu killed King Liao of Wu with dagger hidden in the belly of a fish.

with the sacred task of assassinating the king. Zhuanzhu managed to become one of the king's servants and came up with a remarkable plan to successfully accomplish his mission. At that time servants had to be naked when bringing food to the king's table so Zhuanzhu ingeniously hid his dagger in the belly of a fish, which was being brought to the table as part of a royal feast. As soon as the dish was brought to the king, Zhuanzhu ripped the dagger from the fish's body and plunged it violently into the king's back. Zhuanzhu was immediately hacked to pieces by the king's bodyguards, but he had fulfilled his mission.

Prince Guang had finally become the king of the State of Wu, adopting the ceremonial name He Lü. He took care to honour Zhuanzhu's widow and mother, receiving them respectfully in his capital, the modern day city of Suzhou.

A glimpse of Zhuanzhu Alley.

The assassin's fame lives on in the name of Zhuanzhu Alley, so named because his family lived there, and in the naming of a type of dagger, the Fish Intestine Dagger, in recognition of the ingenuity of Zhuanzhu's assassination. The new king He Lü was to exert a powerful influence on the destiny of the young man recently arrived from the State of Qi.

In the middle of the Spring and Autumn Period (770 BC-476 BC), the states of the Central Plains thought of themselves as the central powers of the land and regarded the people of Wu as barbarians. They failed to appreciate that development in the State of Wu meant that they were rapidly catching up with, and even surpassing, the sophistication and power of the central states. Bronze smelting techniques advanced greatly among the Wu and made them the dominant metalworkers in all the lands. Metalworking skill meant improved swords and improved swords equated to greater military power. The State of Wu advanced rapidly and the beautiful gardens still in evidence in Suzhou today attest to the growing cultural sophistication that went hand in hand with the military development of the state.

In Huqiu, one of Suzhou's noted beauty spots today, there is a place named Sword Pond (Chinese: Jian Chi), where He Lü, the king, is said to be buried. Of the numerous and precious funerary objects

Huqiu Hill Scenic Spot has a history of 2,500 years. It was said to be where He Lü, father of King Fu Chai of Wu, was buried. It is also famous for its "Sword Pond" and the 1,000-year-old Yunyansi Pagoda. September 23, 2006 saw the opening of the Huqiu Temple Fair.

found there, the most valuable were 3,000 fine swords. Qin Emperor Shihuang (259 BC-210 BC), the first emperor of Chinese feudal times, after he had unified the territory of China, ordered his men to make swords just like these but they did not have the craftsmanship and skill of the Wu metalworkers and could not do it.

The prosperity and vitality of the vibrant Wu State proved the perfect environment for a young man full of enthusiasm and ambition - he was Sun Tzu. Sun settled down near Qionglong Mountain not far from the Wu capital and led a quiet, reclusive life. He made no effort at first to seek official position in the Wu administration

Qionglong Mountain, 340 meters high, is the highest peak in the Suzhou area. Hence the other name by which it is known, "First Peak of Wuzhong." Local legend records

Huqiu Sword Pond is where Wu King He Lü was believed to be buried.

that it was in a modest hut in the valley of Qionglong Mountain, that Sun Tzu first lived in the State of Wu. Today, a memorial archway, on which is written four Chinese characters, "兵法圣地" (Bing Fa Sheng Di, meaning "Holy land of Military Tactics"), stands at the gate to this hut, today known as Sun Wu Yuan. According to eminent local scholars, it was in this modest dwelling that one of the masterpieces of the ancient world, *The Art of War*, was produced.

Qionglong Mountain is located at the very centre of the most strategically important area of Wu territory. It is the tallest peak in the region and thus its commanding views were of the utmost military importance. With lush forests, rolling, expansive valleys abounding in clean flowing rivers, and an agreeable climate, the mountain overlooking Lake Taihu offered then, and indeed still offers today, a most attractive environment to live in.

According to the prestigious Chinese

Qionglong Mountain is the highest mountain in the Suzhou area. Its chief peak rises 340 meters. Given this, it was the No.1 strategic high place in war. Here Sun Tzu wrote *The Art of War*.

historical chronicle, the *Spring and Autumn of Wu and Yue*, at that time Sun Tzu withdrew completely from the world. His neighbours all regarded him as an eccentric, whose behavior was puzzling and unconventional. They certainly had not the slightest inkling that here was a man blessed with a genius that would shock the whole world. Living in his little hut, Sun immersed himself in writing his book and simultaneously he kept a close eye on the changing winds of political fortune, carefully calculating the optimum time to emerge and to make his mark in the world of political affairs.

The Wu King He Lü had long nurtured ambitions to carry out a military expedition northwards in order to expand the territory and power of the Wu State. But his first priority was to confront the strong, military power, which was the State of Chu. Chu, a state with a lineage stretching

Working on "The Art of War"

The Art of War Sun Tzu wrote during his hermit life.

Sun Wu Yuan lies in Maopengwu at Qionglong Mountain. Sun Tzu settled down here leading a quiet, reclusive life. He wrote *The Art of War* here.

back almost one thousand years', was an aggressive, expansionist power. It had, during the Spring and Autumn Period (770 BC-476 BC), conquered as many as 45 states, expanding its territory one hundred times over. The Chu were a quintessentially martial and warlike people. It's said that the people of Chu would feel they were shaming their ancestors if they didn't conduct a major military expedition at least every three years and a major war at least every five years.

Why would the State of Wu even countenance attacking such a powerful western neighbour? It seems the main reason lies in a longstanding oppression that the Wu suffered at the hands of the Chu and perhaps more importantly the fact that King He Lü was determined to pursue an aggressively, expansionist military policy.

Thus it came to pass that the State of Wu, in the eastern lands of China, began to inexorably build up and expand its military capabilities under the leadership of an ambitious king, who recognized from

Marble stone wall inscribed with *The Art of War* by Sun Tzu.

the very beginning that dreams of martial glory would remain just dreams for the State of Wu unless the mighty Chu could first be dealt with and defeated. However, the means by which such a seemingly all

powerful force could be militarily defeated by what appeared an inferior power was a conundrum that greatly troubled King He Lü's thoughts.

The Art of War Corridor covers an area of 1,300 square meters. The front wall has black marbles measuring 19.3 meters long and 4.8 meters high, which contain the whole texts of Sun Tzu's *The Art of War*. On its both sides are inscribed with the texts in Japanese and English. Opposite the Chinese texts are carved with inscriptions by modern generals and noted calligraphers.

計篇

曹操曰計者選將量敵度地料卒遠近險易計於廟堂也○李筌曰計者兵之上也太一遁甲先計神加德官以斯主客成敗故孫子論兵亦以計為篇首○杜牧曰計筭也何事曰下之五事所謂道天地將法也於廟堂之上先以彼我之五事計筭優劣然後勝負既定然後興師動眾用兵之道莫先此五事者為篇首耳○王晳曰計者謂計主將天地法令兵賞罰也○張預曰管子曰計先定於內而後兵出境用兵之道以計為首也或曰兵貴臨敵制宜曹公謂計於廟堂者何也曰將之賢愚敵之強弱地之遠近兵之眾寡得不先計之乎兩軍相臨變動相

Ability to Command Troops

As if in answer to his prayers, a great military strategist emerged to provide the King of Wu with the key to his dilemma. This man was Wu Zixu, a former minister of Chu, who had fled to

Wuxiangci Temple built in the Panmen Scenic Area of Suzhou to commemorate General Wu Zixu.

Wu after his father had been killed by the King of Chu. Desperate to avenge his father and escape capture, he traveled down the Yangtze River until he at last arrived in Wu. Because of his bitter enmity towards the Chu king, Wu Zixu was only too willing to assist the State of Wu in their campaign against the Chu.

The Qionglong Mountain recluse, Sun Tzu, had during his time on the mountain struck up a close friendship with Wu Zixu, the exiled Chu minister. Five years later, that same Wu Zixu, when he became the leading minister of the Wu State, had no hesitation in formally recommending Sun Tzu to the king of Wu as a most able candidate for high office. The Qionglong Mountain hermit stepped forward to play a central role in the worldly affairs of men.

The age-old Suzhou City has, since ancient times, enjoyed fame as a paradise on

Sitting statue of General Wu Zixu within the Wuxiangci Temple in the Panmen Scenic Area of Suzhou.

earth, but it is not widely known that the original creator of the paradise is an exile from the State of Chu Wu Zixu. This former general of Chu, who had played a leading role in He Lü's long march to the throne, even finding the assassin Zhuangzhu, and thus effectively bringing about He Lü's rise to ultimate power, was appointed to the very highest office by the grateful king. Wu Zixu's first undertaking as a Minister was to oversee the construction of He Lü City, the city which would eventually become the earthly paradise of Suzhou. Wu Zixu was very much a hands-on city planner: he identified suitable soil as well as tasting the groundwater; he observed the heavenly omens as well as attending to earthly concerns, conducting extensive hydrological and geological surveys of the area.

He had able assistance though. The complex projects to draw water into the city and form an urban chessboard pattern by developing a street system which would run parallel to water channels, was the brainchild of the hermit of Qionglong Mountain, Sun Tzu. At Sun's suggestion,

Wu Zixu ordered the construction of 16 city gates, eight on land and eight on water, spread out around the circumference of the 23.5-kilometer-long city walls. In those days city walls were a city's last line of defence, and needed to be constructed with the utmost care and foresight. They needed to complement the local topography and facilitate the twin functions of allowing for incoming and outgoing traffic, while facilitating the city's security from attack. Today after two and a half millennia have passed, millennia full of the vicissitudes that history and fate bring to all cities under heaven, Suzhou remains in terms of essential location and scale, much as she was designed. She stands as a living testimony to the genius of the two men whose vision and enterprise gave the city life 2,500 years ago: the two immigrants and friends, Wu Zixu and Sun Tzu.

Panmen was the only ancient water-land city gate kept intact today. Built in 514 BC during the Spring and Autumn Period (770 BC-476 BC), it was rebuilt at the end of the Yuan Dynasty (1206-1368). The gate tower was rebuilt in 1986. Complete with heavy sluice gate, it controlled the flow of passengers and ships for defensive purpose.

Wu Zixu, like Sun Tzu, came from a renowned military family, which had produced a number of eminent generals and marshals. He was deeply influenced by the highly developed military culture of Chu, and the historical records attest to his flair for battlefield planning and strategy. And so it came to pass, in one of the great coincidences with which history is dotted, that Sun Tzu, from the northern lands of Qi, and Wu Zixu, from the southern lands of Chu, met by chance in the lands of Wu.

It seems clear that Wu Zixu was a major influence on the military tactics of Sun Tzu. Many of the strategies employed by southern armies differed greatly from those favoured in the north. Thus the meeting of these two great minds created a dynamic

Xitang is an ancient town in Jiashan County, Jiaxing City of Zhejiang Province. It has a history of about 1,000 years. During the Spring and Autumn Period (770 BC-476 BC), General Wu Zixu built water works here.

fusion; a great synergy between northern and southern military tactics, which is encapsulated in Sun Tzu's *The Art of War*. Indeed if one delves deeper, there are many passages from *The Art of War* that reveal the influence exerted on Sun Tzu, not just by Wu Zixu, but also by King He Lü himself who was also a keen student of warcraft.

For instance, as regards the question of when best to attack an opposing force, Wu Zixu observed: "One must not try to intercept the enemy when their banners indicate perfect orderliness. One must not try to pursue the enemy when their movements indicate perfect array." That is to say, one must prepare sufficiently before going to the battlefields. Almost the identical argument is expounded in *The Art of War*.

King He Lü, as mentioned earlier, was a militarist, a politician, and an accomplished monarch who ruled in a most innovative and progressive manner. He had set his ambitious sights on conquering the much more powerful neighbouring Chu state, but lacked the outstanding general who he felt was absolutely essential if the Wu hoped to have any hopes of success. In 512 BC, the third year of He Lü's reign, Wu Zixu came forward to recommend his friend, Sun Tzu, a young military thinker with an excellent pedigree, well versed in astronomy and topography and with an endless supply of resourcefulness. With respectful ceremony Sun Tzu humbly presented King He Lü with the fruits of his period of seclusion in a hut on Qionglong Mountain. It was a 13-bamboo stem text. It would become known as *The Art of War*. It was Sun Tzu's masterpiece, a wholly innovative approach to the dance of death that was, and is, warfare. The king had found his general.

Ability to Command Troops

Wu Zixu introduced Sun Wu to King of the Wu.

The Art of War makes mention of almost every conceivable situation which can occur in the course of a military engagement. The text also considers a whole host of situations which could result from wholly unexpected occurrences. In effect military combat, which had heretofore been, to a large extent, a chaotic and blood-soaked affair became a rational and precise science. It was not at all clear to contemporaries that he author of the *The Art of War* had just laid down the foundation for Chinese military culture. Here stood a callow 25-year-old man, who had never before experienced first-hand a real battle; it seemed absolutely ludicrous, even suicidal, to put an immense array of mounted and foot soldiers under his complete command.

This was the dilemma facing the king. He very much admired the bamboo text on martial strategy but it was nevertheless just

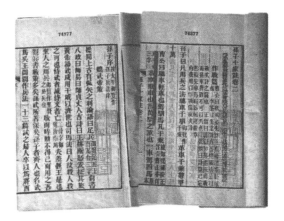

The Art of War.

text'a theoretical treatise with at that time no practical real world application. He Lü was keen to discover to what extent Sun Tzu could apply his theories to the actual battlefield.

The king resolved to test the leadership qualities of the young Sun. Instead of giving him soldiers to command however, the king presented his two favorite concubines. Sun's ability to command them would demonstrate to the king whether or not this young man was charged to command his troops. The two concubines enjoyed the king's favor and thus were most important and privileged personages in court. They looked in contempt at this stripling who thought to command them. When Sun issued them with specific commands and instructions, they mocked him by singing and dancing on the battlefield. It had become a battle of wills and it would end tragically.

Enraged at the attitude of the gorgeous beauties, he ordered his captain to execute them for military insubordination and undermining troop discipline. The ladies were unimpressed by Sun's rage. What could this youth do to the king's favourite bedmates? Sun stood his ground, insisting that since the king had granted him authority he had the right to order the executions.

Ability to Command Troops

Sun Wu beheaded two of the king's concubines in the interest of the Wu State.

Tombs of the two concubines of King of Wu State at the northern slope of Xiaohenshan Mountain in the southern slope of Jiaochangshan Mountain, Xukou of Suzhou.

King He Lü was deeply distressed. He earnestly appealed to Sun: "You have proved your ability to command troops. Please let them go." However, to the king's great disappointment, Sun Tzu refused to back down, insisting that if one wanted to achieve victory, military discipline had to be strictly maintained; since the two courtesans had been designated as Sun

Tzu's troops by the king and since they had committed a grievous breach of military discipline, they must be executed. On the battlefield Sun pointed out as the old maxim went: "A field commander must make the decision even against the orders of the king." The order to execute the concubines was carried out. The king's heart was heavy as his two favourite courtesans were put to the sword but he knew that he now had someone capable of leading his armies; someone who could make his expansionist dreams of conquest come true. Sun Tzu had proved that he had the ruthlessness to lead. The next time he would have real soldiers.

孫子曰

計篇

曹操曰計者選將量敵度地料卒遠近險易計於廟堂也○李筌曰計者兵之上也太一遁甲先計神加德宮以斷主客成敗故孫子論兵亦以計篇為首○杜牧曰計算也曰計算何事曰下之五事所謂道天將法也於廟堂之上先以彼我之五事計算優劣然後勝負既定然後興師動衆用兵之道莫先此五事故為篇首耳○王晳曰計者謂計主將天地法令兵卒賞罰也○張預曰管子曰計先定於內而後兵出境用兵之道以計為首也或曰兵貴臨敵制宜曹公謂計廟堂者何也曰將之賢愚敵之強弱地之遠近兵之衆寡不先計之及乎兩軍相臨變動相

Cream of 'The Art of War'

Thus from 512 BC, Sun Tzu embarked upon the period of his life where he would prove himself as a great military commander. He advised a cautious approach to confrontation with the Chu. King He Lü, as all great rulers must be able to do, heeded the advice of his sage counselor and delayed his intended plan of launching an immediate attack. This phony "War of Cautiousness" lasted a full six years, during which time the State of Wu prepared itself for the coming conflict and also, vitally, rallied to its banner the support of a number of allies, including the States of Tang and Cai. When the armies of Wu eventually set off for battle, it would be as part of a great "multinational" force.

In 1991, almost two and a half millennia after Sun's first northern expedition, another multinational army, before embarking on war in the deserts of Iraq, devoted an enormous amount of time, resources and finances to ensure that when the battle commenced their troops would be absolutely ready and primed for combat. In the ultimate triumph of Operation Desert Storm, which lasted 38 days and cost some US$60 billion, and which saw

Multi-national troops involved in the Gulf War in 1991.

A grand ceremony was held on May 12, 2006 to commemorate the 2,517th birthday of *The Art of War*. Picture shows bamboo slips containing *The Art of War* by offspring of Sun Tzu and the Suzhou Sun Tzu Research Institute.

the Iraqi frontline military forces utterly annihilated, the meticulousness of the pre-war preparations was one of the key contributory factors. The Americans had absorbed well the lessons taught to them by a master of war over 2,000 years dead.

It is amazing to think that a military manual written thousands of years ago at a time when swords and spears and not depleted uranium or Scud missiles were the weapons of war, could retain such relevance for modern military planners. *The Art of War* was written towards the end of the Spring and Autumn Period (770 BC-476 BC), a time of enormous social, intellectual and spiritual ferment in the Chinese lands. The spirit that inspired the wise thought of Lao Tzu, that moved the benevolent heart of Confucius also possessed Sun Tzu and enabled him to set down the basic principles of warfare, which have endured right down to our own day despite the enormous changes that have occurred in the interim.

Near the start of *The Art of War* the central importance of war to the welfare of the State is attested. It is, the author observes, a matter of life and death, a road either to glory and survival or else to defeat and ruin. Thus a state that neglects its attention to warfare risks its entire existence. Nevertheless, Sun Tzu's first actions as a military commander were to avoid conflict to bide his time and ensure that all possible preparations were made. Chinese traditional culture has always stressed the hazards and risks of war and how it should be embarked upon only with very great caution. Although there is no mention of the idea of a "War of Cautiousness" in Sun Tzu's magnum opus, the text is replete with exhortations about the absolute necessity for painstaking preparation. It was to prove a wise tactic.

Sun Tzu always maintained that the greatest victory was one that could be achieved without fighting. Combat for its own sake was not something that he regarded as glorious; war was rather a mere means to an end. He would look aghast at a battlefield drenched with blood where the survivors outnumbered the slain. The killing fields of World War I and much of the 20th century would not have impressed him as proper examples of the way war should be carried out.

This reticence about embarking on war is characteristic of much of traditional Chinese military thinking and is inseparable from traditional farming civilization as practiced in the Chinese

On July 16, 2011, Arsène Wenger, chief coach of the Arsenal Football Club, received a copy of Art of War from the sponsors.

lands. War should never be undertaken on the basis of temporary indignation or the passion of the moment. Human beings are indeed creatures of passion but when emotion is the major factor in any decision, that decision could have disastrous consequences. The example from the Three Kingdoms period when Liu Bei of the Shu Kingdom mobilized a national campaign to avenge the killing of his sworn blood brother, Guan Yu, is a revealing one. It was a decision motivated by passion and grief and it proved a disastrous one because adequate preparation was hopelessly neglected. The end result was the needless deaths of hundreds of thousands of Wu soldiers. These were lessons which had already been taught centuries earlier by Sun Tzu but they had not been learned by Liu Bei and his leadership proved catastrophic for his kingdom.

Liu Bei of the Shu Kingdom led an expedition against Sun Quan of the Wu Kingdom.

In the years after his final defeat at Waterloo, it is reported that the great French general and politician Napoleon Bonaparte got his hands on a French version of Sun Tzu's *The Art of War*. When he read the passage - "No ruler should put troops into the field merely to gratify his own spleen; no general should fight a battle simply out of pique," he is said to have closed the book and heaved a deep sign. "If I could have read this book 20 years ago, all of history may have turned out differently," the exiled former emperor remarked.

This cautiousness about going to war is absolutely central to the ideas and world view of Sun Tzu. "A kingdom that has once been destroyed can never come again into being; nor can the dead ever be brought back to life." Thus the enlightened ruler is heedful, and the good general cautious so that unnecessary loss of life and resources may be avoided. In the passage, *Attack by Stratagem*, Sun observed that the highest form of generalship is to trump the enemy's plans; next best is to prevent the coordination of the enemy's forces; the next best is to attack the enemy's army in the field; worst of all is to besiege walled cities. Thus *The Art of War* is not a glorification of the battlefield and the blood that is spilt on

Children Painting Show titled "War and Peace" was held in Moscow, Russia, on October 5, 2004.

A peace pigeon on the Iraqi battlefield.

it; on the contrary it declares the supreme military achievement to reside in breaking the enemy's resistance without fighting at all. The battle may be won by one's wits and wisdom as much as it may be by sword and shield and indeed the former is to be much preferred.

Even though Sun Tzu is rightly recognized as an outstanding militarist, it is thus not oxymoronic to describe him also as an idealistic pacifist. War may be essential to the well-being of a state Sun taught us, but it should be avoided if at all possible.

During the blood-soaked 20th century, over 130 wars took place, during which some 120 million people lost their lives, a total that is reckoned to surpass the total number of deaths in all wars in history before 1900. Perhaps this is another reason why so many state leaders, militarists and scholars have turned to Sun Tzu's *The Art of War*. Perhaps it reflected a general conviction that in the face of the bloodiest and cruelest century in history, another way needed to be found. The eminent Britain military historian and strategist, Liddell Hart put forward an "Indirect Route

A score of African young generals made a study tour of Sun Wu Yuan in Suzhou on September 21, 2006.

Stratagem" which he openly admitted had been inspired by Sun Tzu's imperatives to "break the enemy's resistance without fighting."

American tactics during the Second Gulf War offer another illustration of the influence of the idea of "breaking the enemy's resistance without fighting." As Sun Tzu explained, "A whole army may be robbed of its spirit; a commander-in-chief may be robbed of his presence of mind." Sun may never have dreamed of an army of such technological and military might as that put into the field by the Americans but he would have well recognized the thrust of their tactics. Their so-called "Precision strikes," and the "media war" that was waged every day gradually sapped the will of the enemy and as resistance steadily crumbled, the war ended quickly with none of the bloody sieges that wad been direly forecast beforehand.

計篇

曹操曰計者選將量敵度地料卒遠近險易計
於廟堂也○李筌曰計者兵之上也太一遁甲先
計神加德宮以斯主客成敗故孫子論兵亦以計為篇
○杜牧曰計算也曰計算何事曰下之五事所謂道
法也於廟堂之上先以彼我之五事計算優劣然後
勝負既定然後興師動眾用兵之道莫先此五
者為篇首耳○王晳曰計者謂計主將天地法令兵
卒賞罰也○張預曰管子曰計先定於內而後兵出
用兵之道以計為首也或曰兵貴臨敵制宜曹公謂計
朝堂者何也曰將之賢愚敵之強弱地之遠近兵之
得不先計之及乎兩軍相臨變動相

Destroying a Superpower

After six years' of careful preparation, the national power of the Wu State had been greatly strengthened and it was now in a position to go to war against the Chu. Sun Tzu and Wu Zixu together formulated a plan to "exhaust and mislead the Chu." The morale of the powerful Chu and its will to resist were gradually undermined and eroded by the Wu force's frequent attacks. At the same time, many Chu allies defected to the Wu side, so that on the eve of war the Wu State effectively controlled the Yuzhang area of the Yangtze River and Huaihe River Valleys which lay between the Wu and Chu States. This would be vital in the coming conflagration.

Sun Tzu's tactics centred around the need

Sun Wu Tzu Pavilion at Huqiu Hill in Suzhou.

to deceive, mislead and above all exhaust the Chu forces. A policy of "Three against One" was adopted, whereby three forces would take turns attacking the enemy who effectively faced a fresh army each time. The army of the Chu State inevitably became exhausted and dispirited.

In the winter of 506 BC, King He Lü personally led an expedition with Sun Tzu and Wu Zixu as his generals. Allied with the States of Tang and Cai, the Wu boasted total forces numbereing some 30,000. Turning from devious to direct tactics, they launched a surprise strategic attack on defences in the north of the Chu State. Under the command of Sun Tzu, the forces of the State of Wu advanced steadily beyond the Huaihe River and began the large-scale destruction of the Chu State in the greatest battles seen in the Chinese lands since the Shang and Zhou Dynasties (16th century BC-256 BC). Sun observed that there was nothing more difficult than tactical manoeuvres, which must be carried out in order to turn from devious to direct tactics.

Destroying a Superpower

Battle fought to defeat the Chu State.

In 1021 BC, or 500 years before the time of Sun Tzu, Jiang Taigong, a founding father of the State of Qi where Sun Tzu's hometown was located, led an army against the King of Zhou. After crossing the Yellow River, they scuttled all available ferries. Later, this army who had cut themselves off from possible retreat, overthrew the Yin and Shang Empires. As Sun Tzu wrote in *The Art of War*: The general must sometimes place his soldiers in danger in order to make them move forward and not withdraw. However, SunTzu's forces didn't destroy the ferries after crossing the Huaihe River and coming ashore at Huangchuan, in Henan Province. Perhaps King He Lü insisted that the possibility of retreat be countenanced and didn't allow it.

After a long march from Suzhou City, the armies of the State of Wu arrived at the banks of the Hanshui River. The river was all that separated them from the capital of the Chu State. The unprepared Chu forces rushed out to confront the Wu armies.

This famous battle which took place 2,500 years ago can be seen as almost certainly the first quasi-naval military engagement, despite the fact that it took place on a river and not at sea. King He Lü, Wu Zixu and Sun Tzu led a great force of soldiers from Taihu Lake, up the Yangtze River, north along the Huaihe River until eventually arriving in the Chu lands.

The army of Chu first tried to outflank the army of Wu and destroy their warships in order to cut the Wu forces off from possible reinforcement and retreat. However, an impatient Chu general called Nangwa didn't allow enough time for his forces to successfully get behind the Wu forces. He desired personal glory and so rashly he led his army across the Hanshui

River to attack the Wu army.

When he saw Nangwa's forces advance across the river, Sun Tzu immediately ordered his forces to pretend to withdraw at once. At Boju at the foot of the Dabieshan Mountain after retreating some hundreds of kilometers, Sun mustered his armies and waited for the enemy.

In ten days in the middle of November in the year 505 BC, with banners and flags unfurled and the drums of war echoing off the verdant hills, the legendary Battle of Boju, the most large-scale military engagement since the Shang and Zhou Dynasties (16th century BC-256 BC), took place. With Dabieshan Mountain at their backs, the Wu armies rushed at the forces of Chu. It was a fierce battle with much blood spilt on both sides, but in the end the 30,000-strong Wu army miraculously emerged victorious against the 200,000

Sun Wu directed the Wu troops to defeat the Chu troops which were numerically superior during the Boju Battle.

The Boju battleground is located inside Macheng City, Hubei Province.

soldiers of the Chu army.

Sun Tzu explained the rationale behind such a battle in *The Art of War*: "Place your army in deadly peril, and it will survive; plunge it into desperate straits, and it will emerge safely." The Battle of Boju was the very zenith of the practical application of Sun Tzu's military thought on the battlefield.

The advance of the Wu armies into

the lands of Chu could not now be stopped. The rampant Wu forces carried all before them. The Chu general Yinshu Shen staged a desperate rearguard action in an attempt to stem the tide but it was to no avail. General Shen died in battle on the very threshold of the state capital. In ten days the Wu armies attacked five times and achieved five crushing victories. The Chu king, Zhao, fled with his retinue to the State of Sui. The forces of the State of Wu entered triumphantly the gates of the Chu capital, Ying. Victory was theirs.

The seemingly invincible State of Chu had been comprehensively overrun and conquered by a numerically inferior force. It is true that the Wu armies were smaller in numbers than those of the Chu, but they were commanded by one of the greatest military minds of all history, Sun Tzu. The war against the Chu marked the coming of age of Chinese military strategy. It was the first recorded example of a military "campaign" in the modern sense of a carefully planned programme of military engagement. The victory was a vindication of Sun's assertion that military triumph comes only with the fusion and cooperation of the talent, wisdom, courage and will of the people of a state. It was also, above all, the supreme vindication of the military theories of a young man from the lands of Qi, Sun Tzu.

To many contemporary observers, the State of Chu had seemed the strongest of all the candidates who might one day unite the fragmented states of the Chinese lands. Thus the unlikely triumph of the Wu can be said to have fundamentally altered the course of Chinese history. Without their victory over the Chu, perhaps Qin Shihuang, cruel originator of the Qin dynasty (221 BC-206

BC) centuries later, would never have risen to power.

There are 13 sections and a mere 5,913 Chinese characters in the book *The Art of War*, but one could say that three sentences and 12 Chinese characters are enough to convey the essential message of the book: "Know your enemy. Know yourself; know the conventions of war but do not fear to transcend them; strike the enemy where they are weakest."

計篇

曹操曰：計者，選將量敵度地料卒遠近險易，計於廟堂也。○李筌曰：計者，兵之上也。太一遁甲先計神加德宮以斷主客成敗。故孫子論兵亦所謂計為篇首。○杜牧曰：計算也。曰計算何事曰下之五事計算優劣然後知勝負既定然後興師動眾，用兵之道莫先此五事。故將法也，於廟堂之上先以彼我之五事計算之，以知勝負，既定然後興師動眾，用兵之道莫先此。○賈林曰：計算者謂計主將天地法令兵眾賞罰也。○張預曰：計為首也。或曰：兵貴臨敵制宜，曹公謂計…用兵之道以計為首也。將之賢愚敵之強弱地之遠近兵之…

Fading from Historical Record

The State of Wu took its place as a major player on the patchwork of fragmented states that inhabited the lands of what is now China. Her eminence would not last long though. In 496 BC, King He Lü died from a sword wound in a battle with the State of Yue. His son Fu Chai succeeded to the throne and, after a two year campaign, succeeded in subjugating the State of Yue. Eager to humiliate his vanquished Yue King Gou Jian, Fu Chai insisted that Gou Jian be his slave, working in the royal stable. Wu Zixu, the wily commander, saw the folly of such a policy and endlessly pleaded with the young king to kill Gou Jian, for only in that way could the final defeat of the Yue forces be utterly

Shaoxing of Zhejiang Province is a famous historical city. About 10 kilometers away from downtown Shaoxing is Shihoushan Mountain, where the defeated King Gou Jian of the State of Yue worked as a slave in the royal stable of King Fu Chai of the State of Wu some 2,000 years ago.

guaranteed. The capricious king flew into a rage and commanded his loyal general to take his sword and end his own life. Once again Wu Zixu had met with the treachery of kings, but this time it would cost him his life. He faced his fate with dauntless valour, asking only that his eyes be cut out before he died and placed on the city walls so that

General Wu Zixu was ordered by the king to die.

he would be able to witness for himself the inevitable destruction of the great power of the State of Wu, which he had done so much himself to bring about.

In 473 BC the dead eyes of Wu Zixu looked on lifelessly as the walls of the last Wu stronghold were razed by the armies of the State of Yue. Military triumph is indeed glorious but the fruits of success do not take long to wither and rot.

Sun Tzu faded quietly from the historical record. Nobody seems to know exactly what became of him. Some contend that he returned to a life of seclusion, disgusted at the idiocy of King Fu Chai's rule. They point to a grave in Wu County in Suzhou City as the great general's final resting place; some believe he himself was a victim of the king's arrogant tyranny. Others say he fought on and vanished during the Yue invasions, others still maintain that he returned to his homeland in the lands of Qi. It seems we can never really be sure.

What is certain is that the 13 bamboo stems left behind by this man who lived over two and a half millennia ago, exerted a profound influence on the course of history

According to historical records, the tomb of Sun Wu is located in Sundunbang, Huxiaocun Village, Yuanhe Town, Suzhou City.

and the philosophy not just of warfare but of all areas of social relations. Sun Tzu is rightfully regarded as one of the greatest minds and theorists in all of Chinese history and civilization.

計篇

曹操曰計者選將量敵度地料卒遠近險易計於廟堂也〇李筌曰計者兵之上也太一遁甲先計神加德宮以斷主客成敗故孫子論兵亦以計為篇首〇杜牧曰計算也曰計算也何事曰下之五事計算優劣然後定勝負既定然後興師動衆用兵之道莫先此五事故為篇首耳〇王晳曰計者謂計主將天地法令兵衆勝罰也〇張預曰管子曰計先定於内而後兵出境故用兵之道以計為首也或曰兵貴臨敵制宜曹公謂計將之賢愚敵之強弱地之遠近兵之

Quotations from Sun Tzu

War Is Closely Related to the Fate of a Country and Its People

War is of vital importance to a country. It is a matter of life and death for the country and its people. Hence it needs careful and cautious investigation and research.

(Military affairs are closely related to politics) Politically, there is unity of will between the people and the king. Both will be willing to risk life and death regardless of the dangers.

Leaders who are skillful at tactics try to

control wars by cultivating a moral law and strictly adhering to rule by law.

They should only act for their own benefit, lead their troops confident they can achieve victory and start wars at the right moment.

The king and his generals should not start a war in anger but rather should fight only if it is in line with national interests and they should desist from fighting if it is not. Rage and anger can turn to joy and happiness, but the country can disappear if it is destroyed and dead people cannot be reborn. Hence, wise kings and excellent generals should be cautious of war, which is only common sense if one wishes to safeguard the country and the army.

☆

Troops should always try to achieve a quick victory because they will be tired and frustrated if they are locked in stalemate for a long time. The army will lose its fighting capacity if it is involved in a tough long drawn out siege of a city. It will inevitably exhaust the country financially if the army has to fight for a very long time.

☆

The country will become impoverished due to war because the war will exhaust the people. Prices will soar near the garrison camp, leading to a depletion of private wealth. If this happens, people will eventually be unable to afford taxes and corvee.

Dispatching a large body of troops to fight far from home will lead to extensive material losses and enormous military spending. Moreover, money has to be spent every day. Soldiers will be exhausted from marching and people will not be able to engage in normal production as the country will be in turmoil.

Wise kings and excellent generals can defeat their enemy as they will gain an understanding of the enemy's situation in advance. They must rely on people who are familiar with the enemy, rather than gods or simply analogies of similar events from the past or superficial evidential data to obtain information about the enemy in advance.

The Cultivation and Role of Generals

A commander skilled at the art of fighting is the arbiter of a people's fate and a country's safety.

Military generals assist in the governance of the country. The country will become powerful if the generals can provide careful and well thought out strategies and the country will become feeble if they fail to perform this role.

A general should neither pursue fame after victory nor evade responsibility after defeat when leading his troops. He should only pursue the interests of the people and the king. Such generals are the most valuable currency for a country.

Military generals should be resourceful, trustworthy, merciful, compassionate, courageous, determined and disciplined.

Soldiers will be confused if a king who doesn't understand military affairs interferes with his command and management of the army. (It's the harm which the king brings to the army)

Victory can be predicted based on the following five circumstances. Those who manage to accurately judge whether it's worth entering the war will win; those who take countermeasures according to an accurate assessment of the enemy forces will win. Those who are supported by all the people and the army will win. Those who are well prepared to fight against an unprepared enemy will win. Those who are capable and do not suffer interference from their king will win.

Not all roads are suitable. Not all enemies should be pursued and attacked. Not all cities should be invaded. Not all regions can be seized. A king's unreasonable orders can very often not be carried out.

People will fight better if they are confident they will achieve victory; if they are not, the people may refuse to fight even if the king orders it.

The man who is short-sighted and arrogant will be captured by his enemies.

Generals will enjoy support from their soldiers by virtue of their erudition and their strict military discipline.

The fact that orders are strictly followed indicates that generals get along well with soldiers.

The most stupid general fears his soldiers after treating them harshly.

A wise general should correctly judge the enemy's situation, study the terrain and accurately assess the distance.

Soldiers will take risks and follow their general if he is as merciful to them as he would be towards his sons.

Soldiers will fight like spoiled children if the general treats them over-kindly without military discipline and punishment when they break rules.

A general who is in charge of military affairs should be calm and wise when making decisions and manage his army impartially and systematically.

It will lead to chaos if a lieutenant launches an attack because of personal resentment going against the orders of his general.

A general who does not train his soldiers properly as a result of weakness will cause problems in the relationship between him and his soldiers. The whole military arrangement will be thrown into disorder and chaos.

The army will be defeated if a general cannot correctly judge the enemy's situation and orders a premature attack against a larger and stronger enemy.

The Overall View of War

The principles of war are as follows: Taking the enemy's country whole and intact is better than defeating it in war; making the whole enemy surrender is better than shattering and destroying them.

The wisest strategy is to defeat the entire enemy force without fighting rather than to insist on a battle each time.

The ultimate goal of conflict is to defeat the enemy with your strategies; an inferior goal is to defeat them through diplomacy; even more inferior is to defeat them in battle; the worst is to invade their cities. Indeed the last choice should be to invade their cities.

One who is skillful in conflict can defeat the enemy without a fight.

The ideal strategy for defeating one's enemy should be a comprehensive, complete strategy, which can avoid the loss of soldiers and gain benefit at the same time.

One who cannot fully understand the damage that war causes can only have a partial knowledge of the profits it can bring.

A wise commander must take the profits and damage into account when considering his strategies. The battle will go smoothly if he considers favorable factors in an unfavorable situation; potential dangers can be eliminated if he considers unfavorable outcomes in what seems favorable conditions.

Careful and thorough planning contributes to victory; failure to plan will lead to failure – one cannot fight, without a plan.

We have heard of the stupidity of haste in war. Cleverness has never been associated with long delays. No country has ever benefited from prolonged warfare.

The most important thing in a fight is to win in a short time so things should never be delayed for too long.

War - The 'Deceptive' Art

All wars are actually based on deception.

A general who wins a war by deceit makes his decisions based on his judgment of whether it is beneficial or not and he deploys or concentrates his forces or changes tactics based on his reading of the situation.

Wars can always be won by fighting

against an enemy using conventional face to face tactics but they can also be won using special tactics.

There are only two main combat tactics, namely, "indirect tactics (special tactics)" and "direct tactics (conventional tactics)", but the combinations of these two tactics are countless. Who can count them as they change into each other as a circle without destination?

When able to attack, we must pretend to be unable; when ready to fight, we must pretend to be unready; when intending to attack a nearby target, we must pretend to attack the far one and vice versa.

Hold out bait to entice the enemy if they are greedy; attack them if they are in disorder; defend your position if they are strong; irritate them if they are easy to be angered; make them arrogant if they are usually humble and cautious; make them tired if they are full of vigor; and separate them if they are united.

Attack unexpectedly the place where the enemy is most unprepared.

Give the enemy the impression you are in confusion when in fact you are perfectly organized; show them fear when you are in fact full of courage; display weakness to the enemy when you are at your strongest.

☆

Those who can mobilize the enemy can make the enemy believe a military situation that does not in fact exist and can attract the enemy using appropriate bait.

☆

Those who are good at fighting can always mobilize the enemy without being mobilized themselves.

☆

One's army should be stationed in the place where the opposing army cannot reach; one's army should attack the place which the enemy least expects.

☆

One's army can win if they attack the place where the army is unguarded. One's army can defend themselves solidly if they defend all places which the enemy may attack.

One's army must know how to defend against a force skilled at attacking and attack against a force skilled at defending.

One's army will benefit if they can use decoy tactics skillfully. Even the most excellent spy cannot learn an army's real condition and even the wisest enemy will struggle to formulate a winning strategy if decoy tactics are well deployed.

The enemy may attack even when its envoys act humble; the enemy may withdraw when its envoy acts tough.

The enemy may well have taken up a strategically crucial location if they keep silent when they are nearby; they may wish to entice your forces forward if they challenge us repeatedly even though they are far away from us.

The enemy must be plotting if they negotiate peace without any preconditions.

Two parties are locked in a stalemate for several years and both seek to make a final bid for victory. If the general fails to attach enough importance to his spies, he will fail because he will be unaware of the enemy's true situation. This is extremely stupid. Such a person is not qualified to be a general of an army.

For a general, spies are vital and they must be very well rewarded. Only wise and farsighted sages employ spies; only compassionate and generous sages can recruit spies; only courageous and careful sages can get information from spies.

Only wise and far-sighted sages employ spies; only compassionate and generous sages can recruit spies; only courageous and careful sages can get information from spies.

We must find out who are the spies sent by the enemy so we can bribe them and turn them, and then send them back as double agents. In this way, they will work for us.

If the wise king and the excellent general can employ those of great intelligence to be spies, they will certainly benefit greatly. This is the key to using military force. Decisions about military action must be based on the information provided by spies.

Knowing about both Ourselves and Our Enemy as well as Owning the Initiative is the Key of Winning the Victory

Knowing about both ourselves and our

enemy, we will be free from danger in every war; only knowing about both ourselves, we will have a win rate of 50 percent; not knowing about both ourselves and our enemy, we will be destined to be defeated.

Having full knowledge of both ourselves and our enemy, we will win the battle; grasp all opportunities and seize the most favorable geographical location. Total victory will be achieved.

With the enemy in exposed terrain and our army well stationed, we can keep our forces concentrated, while the enemy forces have to disperse. (This is provided our army and the enemy are well-matched in military strength) If our military forces are concentrated and the enemies are disperse over ten places, our army will have ten times the military strength of the enemy.

Don't make alliances with principalities unless you know what conspiracies are afoot there; don't march unless you know the topographic distribution of the land in front of you - forest, natural obstacles and swamps; you will never gain a favorable geographical location unless you employ local guides.

Those who are skilled at fighting always first create the conditions for victory and wait for the right opportunities to defeat the enemy.

Not being defeated depends on your

own efforts; defeating the enemy depends on exploitable opportunities offered by the enemy's actions. Therefore, those who are skilled at fighting can only ensure that they won't be defeated; they can't ensure that they will defeat the enemy.

Victory is predictable, but it cannot be demanded by subjective desire. In order not to be defeated by the enemy, rigorous defense is important; to defeat the enemy, powerful attack is important.

Those who are skilled at fighting always remain unbeaten and never miss an opportunity to defeat the enemy.

Generally, those who take to the

battlefield early are full of vigor and initiative; those who take to the battlefield late are tired and passive.

When one's army attacks the enemy, they will be unable to resist because their weak link is being attacked. When one's army retreats, the enemy will be unable to give chase because the army will move at high speed.

Apply Flexible Strategies according to Different Situations

The ways to fight are many and numerous like flowing water. Winning victory based on a study of the enemy's situation is another name for skillful deployment of troops.

A favorable situation is only favorable if one takes flexible measures according to those favorable conditions.

Those skilled at commanding in battle always look for favorable conditions instead of demanding perfection from subordinates. Therefore, they are able to make use of talent and master the overall situation of the war.

Strategies to defeat the enemy are always changing, so flexible strategies must be employed according to the current situation.

The principle that should underlie all combat is: when our military forces is ten times that of the enemy, besiege the enemy; when our military forces is five times that of the enemy, attack the enemy; when our military forces is twice that of the enemy, branch out into two columns to attack the enemy; when our force is weaker than that of the enemy, avoid the battle. Therefore, if the weak party decides to fight to the death, they will inevitably be defeated and captured.

Take an easy victory for example. That you have achieved some minor triumph doesn't mean you have great power; that you can see the sun and the moon doesn't mean you have clear sight; that you can hear the thunder doesn't mean you have good hearing.

When the winning side is fighting, they seem to advance irresistibly - this represents military might.

Effective management of a large force of troops like that of a small force of troops relies on rational organization; effective command of a large force of troops like that of a small force of troops relies on a distinct and efficient command system.

An excellent commander can create a threatening and pressing situation and can launch short but forceful attacks.

The essence of the "art of maneuvering" lies in setting a goal that should be achieved on the battlefield as soon as possible in a roundabout way. This can mean changing a seemingly unfavorable condition into a favorable one.

According to the situation on the battlefield, the army can move quickly like the wind; it can march in a leisurely fashion like an expanding tree line in a forest; it can attack cities and capture territories swiftly and fiercely like blazing fire; it can defend and garrison the land steadfastly like an immovable mountain; it can conceal its military movements secretly like murky clouds that obscure the sun; it can act bravely like an irresistible force.

Since soldiers all obey a unified command, brave officials and men won't advance alone and cowards will never retreat alone. This is the best approach to commanding troops.

We can dampen the morale of the enemy and shake the determination of enemy commanders.

People well versed in the art of war can avoid the enemy's attack and can in turn attack the enemy until its morale fails.

Counter the enemy's confusion with neat and uniform troop arrangements; counter the enemy's restlessness with calmness.

An army can effectively deal with an enemy who comes from afar by taking to the battlefield nearby. It can deal with a hurried and tired enemy with calmness and easiness. It can deal with a hungry enemy by storing enough army provisions for their own forces.

Don't intercept an orderly enemy force; don't attack a well-deployed enemy force.

Don't directly attack an enemy forces which occupies the high ground with its back against the mountains.

Don't track an enemy who pretends to flee; don't storm the elite forces of the enemy; don't be greedy — don't swallow the bait the enemy sends as a decoy; don't engage troops who are retreating to their homes.

Don't completely surround an enemy which is trapped; don't press an enemy who is in a desperate situation.

The correct attitudes of a good commander in war are as follows: Depend on full preparations and the correct arrangement of your army instead of hoping that the enemy won't attack; depend on solid and unassailable defense instead of hoping that the enemy won't attack.

You are wrong if you think that the more

the better when it comes to troops. As long as you don't underestimate the enemy, but rather concentrate on your own forces, ascertain as well as possible the enemy's movements and win trust and support from subordinates, you will win.

Terrain is also vital in any battle.

The best commanders can prevent advance and reserve enemy forces from coordinating with each other. They can prevent main forces and smaller forces from cooperating with each other. They can prevent officers and men from helping each other out. They can prevent upper and lower levels from maintaining contact with each other. They can prevent separated soldiers from regrouping and thus can disrupt the enemy's battle array.

We should capture the enemy's most strategically important locations and possessions, so that they will be at our mercy.

Speed is precious in battle. We should seize the opportunity when the enemy is on the back foot, take unexpected routes and attack at places where the enemy is off guard.

The best commanders can command their troops flexibly like the sacred serpent from legend: if you hit it on its head, its tail will react; if you hit it on its tail, its head will react; if you hit it in its middle, both its head and tail will react.

In an urgent situation, the best commanders must unite officers and soldiers.

General rules for fighting in enemy territory are as follows. The more deeply you penetrate into enemy territory, the more alert and attentive your forces will be; the more shallowly you penetrate, the more distracted the soldier's morale will be.

Soldiers' psychological conditions are as follows. They will try to resist when besieged; they will fight to the death in urgent circumstances; they will obey commands when in the most desperate situations.

Soldiers sent to the most dangerous areas can survive on their wits; soldiers facing mortal peril very often survive finally.

Before the battle, we should be as quiet as a girl in order to make the enemy lower their guard; when in the battle, we should be as swift as the fleeing rabbit so that the enemy has no time to resist us.

After the battle is won and the land and cities of the enemy are captured, we should not immediately reward our officers and soldiers , for this can be very dangerous. The wise king will consider this problem carefully and the best commanders must regard such matters seriously.

图书在版编目（CIP）数据

兵圣——孙子：英文/徐远翔，李京著；王壹晨，王国振译.
— 北京：五洲传播出版社，2014.6
（中国智慧）
ISBN 978-7-5085-2767-3

Ⅰ．①兵… Ⅱ．①徐… ②李… ③王… ④王… Ⅲ．①孙武（前533~?）-传记-英文 Ⅳ．①K825.2

中国版本图书馆CIP数据核字(2014)第111259号

顾　　问：冷成金
作　　者：徐远翔　李　京
译　　者：王壹晨　王国振
封面绘画：郑玉阗
插图作者：王振国
图片提供：CFP　东方IC　五洲传播　紫航文化
出 版 人：荆孝敏
责任编辑：王　莉　韩　旭
特约编辑：王　峰
设计总监：蔡　程
设计制作：邹　红

兵圣——孙子

出版发行：五洲传播出版社
地　　址：北京市海淀区北三环中路31号生产力大楼B座7层（100088）
电　　话：010-82005927，010-82007837（发行部）
网　　址：www.cicc.org.cn
开　　本：32开
印　　张：5
设计承制：北京紫航文化艺术有限公司
印　　刷：北京盛天行健艺术印刷有限公司
版　　次：2014年6月第一版　2014年6月第一次印刷
书　　号：ISBN 978-7-5085-2767-3
定　　价：53.00元